Zen Parent,
Zen Child

Reflections to Help Develop
Peaceful Children

Christian Conte, Ph.D.

ISBN: 0692416838
ISBN-13: 9780692416839

DEDICATION

For Kristen and Kaia

OTHER BOOKS & VIDEOS AVAILABLE

Advanced Techniques for Counseling & Psychotherapy

Life Lessons

Teaching Stories: 53 Bits of Advice, Random Ideas, &
Half-Told Tales to Contemplate & Spark Personal Growth

The Art of Verbal Aikido

The Anger Management Workbook

Keys to a Better Life

Getting Control of Yourself: Anger Management Tools &
Techniques

Whether we realize it or not, our children are always watching.

"Zen is being."

- Ancient Buddhist wisdom

Introduction

After our 9 year-old daughter Kaia read the reflections in this book, she looked at me and said, *"Daddy, that had to be the easiest thing you ever wrote."* I spent a lot of time meditating and reflecting to come up with these statements, so I admit I was a little taken back by her statement; but I love her feedback and learn from her constantly, so I asked her to tell me what she meant. *"Well, everything in there is just how you parent. You just wrote down everything you do with me. I bet that was easy!"* she replied. Her answer certainly brought me a welcomed sigh of relief. I smiled and thanked her.

My daughter is very peaceful, loving, kind, compassionate, and happy; but all children have the potential to exude those qualities. As parents, it is our responsibility to guide our children in that direction. Parenting is not complex, but it takes enormous effort;

that is, until you begin to understand Zen – then parenting becomes effortless.

I'm a psychotherapist who has spent the last 17 years working with countless parents and children. I have seen so many families struggle and so many parents make their lives considerably more difficult than they need to be. To help, I created the Four Cs of Parenting so parents could understand exactly how they can approach literally every situation with their children.

The Four Cs of Parenting

My Four Cs of Parenting are: Choices, Consequences, Consistency, Compassion.

Simply put, if you are a parent, you can significantly reduce your own stress and drastically improve your children's lives by following the Four Cs. To begin, the first "C" stands for *choice*. Give your children choices, because choices begin to teach them about the fundamental rule of free will: We always have a choice. Additionally, by providing choices for your children, you are better preparing them to face the innumerable choices that life will bring to them. The more they practice decision-making, the better they get at it. The choices we make in life, after all, help define our legacies, so grant your children choices in all situations, but always hold close what follows those choices: Consequences.

The second "C" stands for *consequences,* because it is

only through consequences that we learn. Way back in the 19th century, the psychologist Edward Thorndike became known for his *law of effect*. Basically, the law of effect is this: If we do something and like the results (consequences), we are likely to do it again; but if we do something and do not like the results (consequences), we are not likely to repeat that behavior. In short, psychologists have known since the inception of the field of psychology that consequences are vital to learning.

The consequences that you provide your children should mirror the type of consequences the world will bring to them. They do not need to be severe because their only intention is *to teach a lesson*. Consequences need to match the choice that was made; which means while ineffective choices can certainly lead to negative consequences, effective choices should lead to positive consequences. All choices that we make in life have consequences, and the earlier your children learn that, the more prepared they will be. Consequences should not be dealt out of anger, because the point of providing them is to help your children learn. The most effective consequences are those that successfully teach your children about the world in which they will live.

Once consequences have been provided, it is time to adhere to the third "C": *consistency*. It is essential that you attempt to be as consistent as possible by following through with the consequences. When parents give in on or otherwise change the consequence in some way, children learn that their parents' word is not to be taken at face value, and they become confused. By being inconsistent, parents encourage their children to repeatedly ask for things or otherwise nag them, and then, interestingly enough, they get angry with their children for doing what they taught them to do in the first place.

Providing choices, implementing consequences, and following through with consistency are all profoundly important; but all combined pale in comparison to the significance of the fourth "C": *compassion*. Without compassion, our children learn to be defiant, angry, resentful, jealous, bitter, and callous. When we provide compassion, however, our children see all the beauty that our species has to offer.

When you truly understand that your job as a parent is *to teach*, compassion will flow through you naturally. The word *education* stems from the root *ducere*, which means "to lead," and the prefix *ex* or *ed*, meaning "out." Education literally means "to lead out;" and if we are helping lead a person out of darkness, then how will it help our purpose to be mad at them for being in the darkness in the first place? When we understand education is about shining light for others, we no longer need to be upset if they "don't get it," and instead we can teach with compassion to help them learn. Out of compassion, after all, comes patience.

As the well-known axiom goes, *children learn more by what they observe than by what they hear*. Therefore the most effective delivery system of the Four Cs is through the medium of role modeling. The sum of parenting is teaching, and I believe the most effective teachers are mindful, reflective role models. The essence of the Four Cs of Parenting is Zen: If you want your children to be peaceful, then you must be peaceful yourself. The same is true of self-discipline, love, kindness, and every other quality. I invite you to draw on the following reflections as a way to remind yourself that your children are watching you in every moment. When you wholly understand the title, *Zen Parent, Zen Child*, you will be fully prepared to help guide your children to a loving, peaceful existence.

REFLECTIONS

1

What you teach your children, they will learn. You know that, of course, but what you might not realize is this: Your children are watching absolutely everything you do. You are teaching in every moment. You are teaching when you least expect it. As a parent, you are a permanent teacher whether you like it or not and whether you believe you "signed up" to be or not. You are your children's teacher; this is truth.

2

Your children will show you who you are. From the moment they see you, your children begin to emulate your facial expressions. As they grow, your children come to say and do what you yourself have said and done. You can hear your accent in your children's voices. You can hear what words you emphasize. Observe your children and see whom you've become.

3

Show your children compassion in every moment. Set your children up in an environment that promotes peace. Surround them with loving images. Love them enough to set boundaries on what you permit them to do. If you allow your children to watch anger and ugliness, then you will have helped to create anger and ugliness in them. Be mindful of this and show your children compassion in every moment.

4

Be a role model who is worth observing. Show your children that you love them enough to demonstrate a balanced lifestyle and healthy habits. Care about your children enough to take care of yourself, so that they in turn learn to take care of themselves. Practice meditation so that your children will practice meditation. In this way you will role model the self-control you want them to have.

5

Try the things you want your children to try. Ask of them the things you are willing to do yourself.

6

Have the self-discipline to be patient. Your children can learn anything. If they do not learn what you want them to learn, it is not their failure to grasp, but your failure to teach in a way that works for them. In regard to your effort, if one way of instruction does not work, try another way; if that method fails, continue trying different ways. Never give up on your children's ability to learn because of your shortcomings as a teacher.

7

Your children will become what you teach them to become. They will be interested in what you are, and they will learn to see the world the way you do. If you are not affectionate, they will suffer. If you are not kind, they will learn that way. If you want them to become something great, have patience with them through their mistakes.

8

Do not be angry with your children for doing what you've taught them to do. If you yell, do not get angry when your children yell. If you use expletives, do not get angry when they use expletives. If you complain, do not get angry when they complain. Be mindful that your children are simply living how you have taught them to live.

9

Do not play the helpless victim when your mistakes are pointed out. You are not the worst parent in the world, but you are not perfect, either. Become a better parent every day by learning from your mistakes. Find the courage to accept feedback and gain wisdom by learning from it.

10

Do not play the role of martyr with your children. Your children are not there to make you feel good. You are there to take care of their needs, regardless of glory, praise, or acknowledgement. True parents do for their children for the sake of doing, not recognition.

11

Make your word your bond with your children. If you say you will play with them, play with them. If you say you will take something away from them, stick to your word. Your children learn about you by observing the degree to which you follow through with what you say.

12

Speak kindly to your children at all times. If you believe, "*I speak kindly to them most of the time*," then that means there are times when you are not kind to them. If there are times when you are not kind to them, then how can you be angry with them if there are times they are not kind in return?

13

Avoid being a hypocritical parent. Hypocritical parents have no patience for their children's mistakes. Hypocritical parents fail to see their own mistakes; or worse still, they acknowledge their mistakes yet continue to repeat them. Hypocritical parents do not recognize that it has sometimes taken them hundreds of times to get a lesson, and so they expect that their own children should get lessons faster. In that way, hypocritical parents have no patience.

14

Give your children *choices* in everything they do because the world will give your children choices in everything they do. Provide *consequences* for the choices your children make because the world will do so as well. Be *consistent* in following through with the consequences because the consequences life brings them will be upheld. Do all three with loving-kindness because the world will not always be compassionate to your children, but you can be.

15

There is a "Thinking" center in the brain and there is an "Emotional" center in the brain. You want your children to learn with the thinking part of their brain, yet when you stand overtop of them, yell at them, threaten them in any way, or otherwise intimidate them, it causes them fear – and fear is in the emotional center of the brain. If you want your children to learn, talk calmly to the thinking center of the brain. If you cannot teach them in the correct part of their brain, then do not be angry with them when they do not understand your lesson.

16

If you act in lazy ways, your children will act in lazy ways. Do not be perturbed when your children do what you modeled for them to do.

17

Give explanations to your children for your decisions. Do not justify yourself but allow them to understand your reasoning. Clarify your intentionality so that they may fully grasp the lesson you want them to learn. If you do not give them explanations, then do not expect them to understand.

18

Have the awareness to recognize that what has worked for you will not necessarily work for your children. Be secure enough in yourself to provide them the space they need to develop in ways that are best for them, even if those ways differ greatly than your own.

19

Your children are not your source of self-esteem. Be your own source of self-esteem. Have the discipline to look inward and the strength to learn about yourself. Learn from your mistakes, grow from them, and do not repeat them. In this way, your own self-esteem will elevate, and in turn, your children will learn how to develop their own sense of value.

20

Remain awed by your children long after they make mistakes. Children are equally as Divine when they mess up as they are when they do well. It is always an honor to be a parent to your children.

21

Allow your children to see that you, too, are still learning. Look at mistakes and obstacles as opportunities to learn and grow; and they, too, will learn to look at mistakes and obstacles as opportunities as well.

22

Know always that your children see your actions, not your intentions. In this way, do not tell them what you "meant" or "did not mean" to do. Instead, show them what you actually meant by your actions.

23

Smile at your children before they go to bed. Smile at your children when they wake up each day.

24

Teach your children that all things change and that some sadness is inevitable. Grant them access to seeing you in times of sadness but go through your sadness with consciousness. *"I am sad,"* tell them, *"but it is okay to be sad. We must sometimes go through the sadness on our way to joy."*

25

Make yourself worth your children's wanting to be around you. No material gifts can match the gift of being a source of peace for them.

26

Teach your children to learn from their dreams. Help them to see that dreams cannot hurt them, only teach them. Help them to gain awareness that dreams speak in symbols, and symbols are designed to evoke thought. Teach them to analyze their dreams and learn from them.

27

Love your children enough to say "No" when it is appropriate. Do not give in to allay your own guilt; instead, always do what is best for your children.

28

Make time to look your children in the eyes every time you are in their presence.

29

Be easy on your children when accidents arise. You wanted as much from your own parents when you were young....

30

Value all your children say. The time you get to hear your children speak is limited. All things are impermanent, but if you listen closely, you can hear the infinite Divine in every syllable uttered from their voices.

31

Accept change so that your children will come to accept change. Without your guidance, changes can halt their lives; with your guidance, they can learn to flow as the river water with change.

32

Align your expectations with reality so that your children can learn to do the same. In this way, they will find balance in all situations.

33

Watch how your children respond to discomfort and disappointment; in so doing, you can see how you respond to discomfort and disappointment. Listen closely to your children and you will hear yourself.

34

Sing to your children even if you cannot carry a tune. Sing to them to show them there is a lighter side to life. Sing to them to bring them warmth and comfort. Sing to your children.

35

Your children are like your garden. You will reap what you sow. Plant love as you would plant your favorite food. Nurture them with kindness and care. Tend to them every single day.

36

Do not get angry when your children get angry because anger cannot be eradicated with anger. If you hope to transform your children's emotions, do so by being a source of peace for them.

37

Meditate every day with your children. In this way you will help them learn the patience you wish for them to have. Do not make excuses for why you cannot find even two minutes to do so; simply make two minutes every day to meditate with your children until you can make more time to do so.

38

Show your children the peace you want them to exude. Avoid simply telling them what not to do and provide them daily instruction on what they can do.

39

Parents who handle their own stress well have children who in turn learn to handle stress well. Therefore, even in the most difficult of times, consider your reaction for your children's sake.

40

Dance with your children even if you cannot dance. As you dance, you spread joyful energy.

41

Show your children the love that you feel. Do not
assume they are assured of your love; instead, find your
own unique ways to demonstrate your love every day.

42

Take the time to figure out the ways in which your children learn best. Some children are visual learners, some learn by listening, still others learn best through experience. Figure out how your children learn best; then go teach them in that way.

43

Expend the effort to know where your children are, whom they are with, and what they are doing. More still, take the time to learn what others are teaching them.

44

Children learn what they see; therefore, be mindful of
what you allow your children to see. If you allow them
to watch violence, they will learn violence. If you
surround them with peace, they will learn peace.

45

Communicate with your children in the mediums they use. Take the time to educate yourself in the ways your children communicate with others and then care enough to meet them where they are.

46

Provide your children with responsibilities so that they learn what it means to be responsible. Do not enable them to be indolent and then question how they have come to be so. Give your children responsibilities that fit their stage of development, provide explanations for why you are doing so, and encourage them with love to embrace their tasks.

47

Teach your children the importance of strengthening their bodies and minds by constantly strengthening your own body and mind. Do so with balance so that they may, in turn, learn balance.

48

Validate your children's emotions. Do not tell them
what they are feeling. Do not demand that they hasten
feeling better so your own needs are met. Instead,
provide a safe space for your children by validating their
feelings until they have helped themselves work
through any troubling emotions.

49

Allow your children to see that you are proud of them simply for breathing. In this way, you will show your children that your love is not conditional and dependent on their achievements.

50

Listen to your children with your eyes as well as your ears. When they see you engaged, they learn to be engaged.

51

Do not make excuses to your children for your mistakes. Instead, accept full responsibility for your actions and treat your mistakes as opportunities to learn.

52

Teach your children to look at the sky and the stars. Regularly, remind your children of the vastness of the universe. In this way, you can help your children develop perspective on the struggles they face.

53

Educate your children about the ways in which things like hunger, fatigue, and body temperature impact their emotions. Role model for them how to handle physical discomfort with grace and calm.

54

Read to your children. Read them peaceful stories that fill their minds with peaceful thoughts.

55

Help your children practice the ways in which they can handle conflict. Role-play potential situations and practice them over and over again. In this way, you will help your children to be more prepared for the difficulties they will encounter.

56

Be mindful that your children are listening to how you speak to other adults. They hear your tone of voice, emphasis, and your language. If you gossip with others, they will learn to do the same. Conversely, if you are conscious in your speech, your children will mimic that as well.

57

Teach your children that they are more than anything they ever do. They are more than their thoughts. They are more than their emotions. They are more than their actions. Teach them that the world will see their actions and judge them accordingly, but you will always see their essence.

58

Know that your children see your actions, not your intentions. Have the strength, courage, and humility to accept feedback from your children. Constantly strive to become a better parent by being open to how your children perceive you; and then improve your actions to better meet your good intentions.

59

Show compassion and respect to those who trouble you. When your children see you doing so, they can learn to do the same.

60

Make your home a place of peace for your children.
Outward chaos can translate to inward chaos;
therefore, make the effort to keep your home a haven
for a quiet mind.

61

Gratitude transforms lives. Express gratitude in front of your children every day. Be grateful for your children, your senses, and your ability to breathe. Express gratitude constantly in your mind and show gratitude daily in your actions.

62

The wicked acts of others stem from pain and never need to be taken personally. Those who are truly peaceful do not hurt others. Therefore, take the time to explain to your children that people hurt each other because they are suffering in some way.

63

Teach your children that suffering stems from desire.
Demonstrate to them that you can control your own
suffering when you control your desire.

64

You can gain awareness regarding how controlling you are by observing the degree to which your children turn to you for approval before answering others. The more your children look to you before they answer others, the more controlling you are, and the less you have helped them achieve independence.

65

If you want your children to learn to not take things so seriously, then you will have to take yourself lightly.

66

Teach your children that what they tell themselves influences how they feel. If they say a situation is "terrible," then they will likely feel inner turmoil; if, on the other hand, they describe the same event as "unfortunate but manageable," then they will likely feel empowered to handle the situation. Teach your children to control their self-talk by the way that you control your own.

67

Invite your children to question the lessons you teach. When they challenge your teachings, offer them explanations. If you cannot offer an explanation, then strongly reconsider what you have taught.

68

Teach your children compassion by seeing the world through others' perspectives. Do so in your own conflicts, and your children will begin to do so in theirs.

69

Love your children enough to be interested in wanting to improve yourself every day for them.

70

Show your children how to start out on a journey and provide them the tools necessary to continue the journey regardless of the obstacles they will certainly encounter.

71

Show your children that you are open to being wrong and excited to learn from every experience. In this way, your children will learn that *not* knowing is merely an opportunity to learn.

72

Teach your children that while those who live in the past are doomed to sadness and those who live in the future are doomed to anxiety, those who live in the present find true peace. Then, you yourself focus less on the past and future and live fully in the present moment.

73

Eat when you are hungry. Sleep when you are tired. Be kind when you interact with others. Put your best effort into all you do. Become who you are destined to become, and your children will do the same.

74

Help your children learn that everything they eat impacts their bodies in some manner. Take the time to teach them the importance of healthy food and make the effort to motivate them to eat well; but grant them the freedom to have their own tastes.

75

Respect all life forms and teach your children to do the
same.

76

Whether you call your children "little buddhas" or "little demons," they will strive to become what you tell them they will be. It is not enough to call your children "little buddhas" only once or only after they have shown kindness; you must define them as such regardless of their mishaps. In this way, you will direct them to become peaceful beings.

77

Have genuine gratitude for everything you receive. By doing so, your children can witness the gratitude you want them to exude.

78

Help your children learn that clear goals are much more likely to be met than unclear goals. Let them know that while anything is possible, everything becomes more achievable with a clear plan and dedication. Lead them to this knowledge by being a living example.

79

Set firm boundaries for your children and be kind and compassionate as you follow through with consequences. In this way, they will learn that their actions have consequences, but experiences are their teachers as well.

80

The more aware you are that the words you say are like boomerangs that will return to you, the more prepared you will be to speak to your children.

81

Spend time laughing with your children every day.

82

When you are rigid, your children become rigid. Life is not a separation of either/or; it is an amalgam of both/and.

83

Change is inescapable. When you can flow with change, your children will, too.

84

It is a huge responsibility to have a conscious child and it takes a tremendous amount of effort; that is, until you understand Zen, then it takes no effort at all.

85

Teach your children that memory is not always accurate. Teach them to eschew saying, *"You said"* in favor of *"I thought I heard you say."* The difference is subtle but profound. Do so by doing so yourself.

86

Impart to your children that each day brings new hunger. As long as they are alive, they will never have *done* enough since there is more to do; but they will always *be* enough.

87

Love your children enough to allow them the space to
live their own lives. Your children are not your property.
Their lives are not meant to complete all you left
undone. Their path is theirs, as yours is yours.

88

Regardless of any circumstance, as long as we are alive, we have our breath. Those who can control their breath can control their thoughts. Help your children become mindful of their breath.

89

We see what we look to see in the world. When we prepare ourselves to see others' struggles, we see their struggles. When we prepare ourselves to see their offenses, we see their offenses. What we see, in turn, shapes us. Teach your children this lesson.

90

When your children feel misunderstood, they suffer.
Put your own needs to be heard aside and seek first to
understand your children.

91

It doesn't matter how you have ever parented in the past; it only ever matters how you parent from this moment forward.

92

Do every task you undertake with honor. Show your children by example that every action you perform is equally important. You will be pleased when they begin to reflect your actions, but do not expect that their life changes should occur when yours do. After all, you are much older than your children and have taken significantly more time to be in this place.

93

Practice with your children the way in which you want them to respond to discomfort. Practice it a hundred times with them. Practice it in times of comfort.

94

When you take your children's mistakes and struggles personally, you mislead them. Their struggles are theirs as yours are yours. Provide consequences and offer love and support, but grant them the respect of their individuality.

95

It is not your children's responsibility to make you feel better simply because it hurts you to see them sad.

96

The thoughtful teaching of a single child can reverberate to multitudes. Know then that when you impact your children, you affect many more; and be mindful that the masses will hear even the whispers you give to your children.

97

You do not own your children. Your children are not your identity. Find completeness in yourself, and your children will do likewise.

98

Teach your children that everything has a season. The easy, the difficult, the sad, and the joyous: they all come and go. Prepare your children.

99

Without attachment to the path you take, your children cannot rebel against your way.

100

If your children express fear or sadness, and you do not believe them, you will teach them to mistrust their emotions. Validate every emotion your children express, and in so doing you will teach them to accurately identify their feelings.

101

Make the effort to help your children spend time in nature. Allow them to connect with the forests, streams, mountains, valleys, plains, caves, deserts, and oceans. Help them see they are a part of the vast world in which they live.

102

If you tell your children they are fine when they insist that they are not, your children become confused. Do not downplay your children's pain because you do not want it to be so. Instead, acknowledge their pain and offer to sit with them. Say, "*I am here if you need me*," and then provide them space to experience their lives.

103

Make plans but be open to changing them. In this way your children will learn the value of nonattachment.

104

If you concern yourself with petty things, your children will as well. Transcend pettiness by maintaining focus on what matters most.

105

Cluttered surroundings clutter minds; therefore, help your children live free from clutter, and teach them the value of a clear space. It might take many teachings to impart this lesson, so be patient and kind.

106

If you consider your children "bad," it is your job to help them become what you consider "good." Neither your sleep nor your entertainment should precede this task.

107

Know that there is no shortcut to helping your children improve on that which needs developed. Demonstrate self-discipline through patience, compassion, and kindness as you guide them toward improvement.

108

There are no heroes, doctors, medicine, teachers, role models, or peers who will have a greater impact on your children's development than you. The *kind* of impact you have is up to you.

109

Ancestors repeated unhealthy patterns simply because they were difficult to break. Therefore, have the fortitude to break tradition and create healthy patterns for your children, as well as their descendants.

110

Use words to tell your children what you want them to learn. Use actions to teach your children by example.

111

Always correct your children with love.

112

Throw the words, "*I already told you*," out of your vocabulary. If you are repeating yourself to your children, you are doing so because they need more time to learn the lesson you are attempting to teach. Be easy on your children in these times because you, too, have experienced lessons that took many years to grasp.

113

Teach your children that if they conquer multitudes it would mean significantly less than if they conquered themselves. Demonstrate to them your own pursuit of conquering yourself.

114

Make meditation the first thing your children do each morning. In this way, you will help them begin their day in peace.

115

Be confident in showing your children the right path
and be kind in the way that you reprimand them. In
doing both you will avoid power struggles, and teaching
will be your goal.

116

As long as you look to your children for fulfillment, you will never be fulfilled. Find fulfillment in your own life, and your children will do likewise.

117

Your job is not to control your children's thoughts but to shape their behavior. Therefore, do not be attached to their opinions and instead always seek to guide their actions.

118

Teach your children to find their own happiness by discovering that true happiness comes from within.

119

Show moderation in what you undertake, say only what you mean, and seek balance. Your children will observe this and learn well.

120

Take the time to light a candle and burn incense before your daily meditation with your children. In doing so, you will teach them to slow down and be present.

121

Embrace the gifts that have been bestowed upon you and avoid greed; in this way, your children will observe contentment.

122

Draw on self-discipline to create change in your family. Allow your children to see that you work persistently on your self-control.

123

When you view parenting as sacred, all moments with your children become important.

124

The more attached you are to being right, the more your children will be as well. Abandon the need to be right, and in so doing, you will teach your children that it is better to be happy than right.

125

Teach your children to be mindful that they are not their emotions, and teach them by understanding this yourself.

126

There will never be a time you regret showing your children love; show your children violence, however, and you will befriend regret forever.

127

No matter how great or trivial the task, put right effort into all you undertake, and your children will learn to do the same.

125

Show your children that, like you, they are and are not the center of the universe. When you fully understand this, they will be a step closer to understanding it as well.

126

Become a Zen parent and you will see your Zen child.

ABOUT THE AUTHOR

Christian Conte, Ph.D. is a parent. He is also a licensed professional counselor and nationally certified psychologist. Dr. Conte is the creator of the Four Cs of Parenting, and the author of several books, including: *Advanced Techniques for Counseling and Psychotherapy*; *Life Lessons*; Teaching Stories; *The Anger Management Workbook*; *The Art of Verbal Aikido*; *Keys to A Better Life*; and the popular video, *Getting Control of Yourself*. You can see him on the show *Coaching Bad* on Spike network and you can learn more about him at **www.DrChristianConte.com**